energy

621

~~GRANDTULLY~~
~~PRIMARY SCHOOL~~

"Kenmore Primary School"

energy

Future Energy Possibilities

Editor: John Clark
Editorial Planning: Clark Robinson Ltd
Design: David West
 Children's Book Design
Illustrator: Peter Harper
Picture research: Cecilia Weston-Baker
Photographic Credits:
Cover and pages 9 both and 25: Science Photo Library; pages 4-5, 7 both, 14,
17 bottom and 19: Zefa Picture Library; page 12: Central Electricity
Generating Board; page 13: ETSU/Harwell; page 17 left: J. Allan Cash
Library; pages 17 right and 26: Davidsons Ltd; page 20: Ford Motor
Company; page 21 top: SERI; page 21 bottom: Lupe Cunha; page 23: The
National Grid; page 24: British Nuclear Fuels Ltd.

Created and designed by
Aladdin Books Ltd
28 Percy Street
London W1P 9FF

First published in
Great Britain in 1990 by
Gloucester Press
96 Leonard Street
London EC2A 4RH

ISBN 0-7496-0370-4

Printed in Belgium

The publishers would like to acknowledge that the photographs reproduced
within this book have been posed by models or have been obtained from
photographic agencies.

A CIP catalogue record for this book is available from the British Library

Facts on

Future Energy Possibilities

Hugh Johnstone

GLOUCESTER PRESS
London · New York · Toronto · Sydney

CONTENTS

Reserves of coal, oil and natural gas are still sufficient to supply the world's energy needs for the present, but they are being used up rapidly. Future demand for energy is expected to be even greater, as developing countries move towards the energy consumption levels of industrial societies. In order to meet these future needs, we have to start investigating and developing alternative energy sources now. It is important that new sources of energy are fully operational by the time we need them. Ideally, these new sources will be non-polluting and renewable – providing a constant supply that will not run out. Possible solutions to the problem are examined in this book. Some of them are already in use, while others are still just ideas and they may never prove practical.

◁ Geothermal station, New Zealand

HOW WE USE ENERGY

Energy is something we use all the time, almost without thinking about it. It comes in many different forms and has many different uses. For example electricity is used for light and heat, gas for cooking, and petrol for running a car. Without energy, it would be impossible to live as comfortably as we do. But the energy we use in our homes is just part of the story. In industrialised countries, domestic users account for only about a third of total energy consumption; the rest is used for industry and transport. Most of the energy we use today comes from burning coal, oil and gas – known as fossil fuels. We need alternatives to fossil fuels partly because they are starting to run out, but also because they cause pollution and damage the environment.

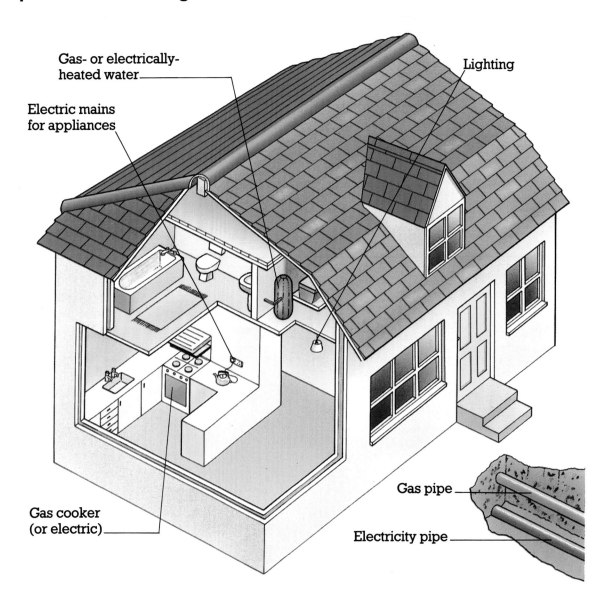

Gas- or electrically-heated water

Lighting

Electric mains for appliances

Gas cooker (or electric)

Gas pipe

Electricity pipe

▽ Nuclear power could meet most of the world's future energy needs, because there is an almost unlimited supply of uranium, which is used as fuel. But there has been much opposition to nuclear power because of the risks involved. An accident could release large amounts of dangerous radiation. The safe disposal of nuclear waste is also a problem, as it remains radioactive for a very long time.

▽ Fossil fuel power stations that burn coal, gas or oil produce most of our electricity. But the vast quantities of fumes that are produced contain substances that pollute the environment, causing problems such as acid rain.

FUSION

Fusion is the process that produces the heat of the sun. The nuclei (central cores) of small atoms join together to form larger nuclei and at the same time produce heat. Nuclei usually repel one another if they get too close, but if the temperature is high enough, atoms are converted into a plasma. In a plasma, nuclei lose the electrons that surround them and move fast enough to collide. Fusion can then take place. But a temperature of about 100 million degrees centigrade is needed, so it is very difficult to create and control a plasma. At the moment, experimental reactors use up much more energy than they produce. But if fusion can be controlled, it will provide a very long-lasting source of energy with relatively little pollution.

INSIDE A REACTOR

The nucleus of ordinary hydrogen contains only a proton. In a reactor, special forms (isotopes) of hydrogen called deuterium and tritium are used. These have neutrons as well. They combine to form a helium nucleus, a spare neutron and energy.

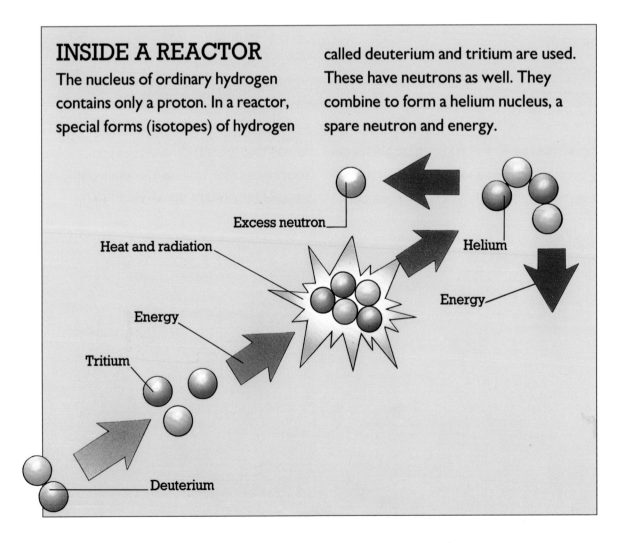

Excess neutron

Heat and radiation

Helium

Energy

Energy

Tritium

Deuterium

TOKOMAK FUSION

The plasma is contained by a ring of magnetic fields. This keeps it from touching the walls, which would cool it down. Lithium is pumped round to trap the heat.

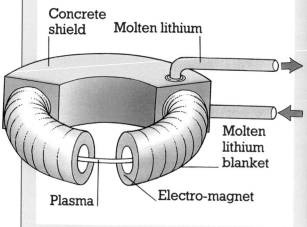

Concrete shield · Molten lithium · Molten lithium blanket · Plasma · Electro-magnet

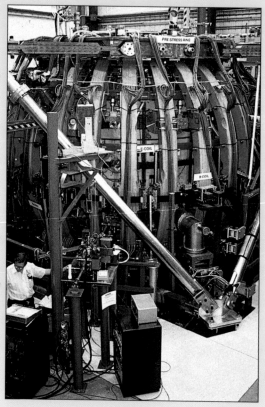

LASER FUSION

Fusion can be started with heat from high-power lasers. The lasers are focused on a minute deuterium fuel pellet, which is dropped in so it does not touch the walls.

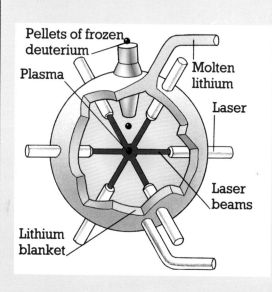

Pellets of frozen deuterium · Plasma · Molten lithium · Laser · Laser beams · Lithium blanket

OCEAN POWER

Oceans cover about two-thirds of the Earth's surface. This water is constantly moving because of the tidal flows, massive ocean currents and waves. The power of these movements comes from the heating effect of the Sun, together with the gravitational pulls of the Moon and the Sun. All such motion could be harnessed to provide useful energy – the deep sea currents alone have a flow many times greater than all of the Earth's rivers. The ocean also acts as a huge thermal reservoir, soaking up the Sun's heat. Around a quarter of the heat reaching the Earth from the Sun goes to evaporate water, which condenses and returns to the Earth again as rain. The water will eventually flow into rivers, and can then be used for hydroelectric power.

RELYING ON THE CURRENT

Groups of several hundred turbines, each more than 150 metres in diameter, could be positioned in large ocean currents, such as the Gulf Stream. The electricity produced would be carried to the shore through underwater cables.

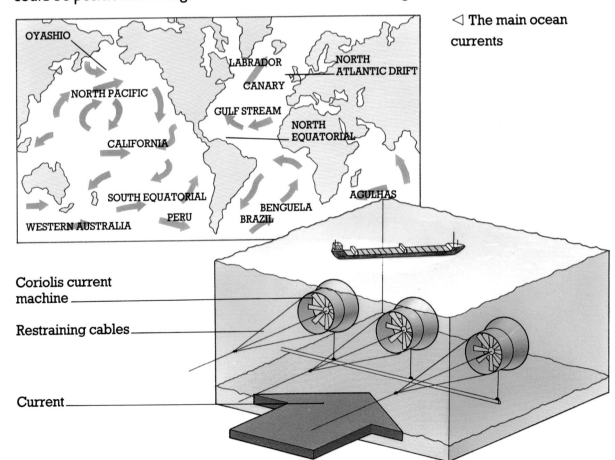

◁ The main ocean currents

OYASHIO

LABRADOR

NORTH ATLANTIC DRIFT

CANARY

NORTH PACIFIC

GULF STREAM

CALIFORNIA

NORTH EQUATORIAL

SOUTH EQUATORIAL

AGULHAS

BENGUELA

PERU

BRAZIL

WESTERN AUSTRALIA

Coriolis current machine

Restraining cables

Current

OCEAN THERMAL

In tropical areas, the Sun's heat only reaches the top layer of the sea, so the water at the surface may be 20 degrees centigrade warmer than the water lower down. Ocean Thermal Energy Conversion (OTEC) systems use this temperature difference to generate electricity. The warm surface water is passed through evaporators to heat a liquid with a low-boiling point, such as ammonia. The heat converts the ammonia into a vapour, which drives a turbine to generate electricity. After passing through the turbine the vapour is condensed using the cold water from the lower levels of the sea. Condensing the vapour gives a lower pressure at the turbine outlet, so the vapour is sucked through and the turbine operates more efficiently. The condensed ammonia is pumped back to the evaporators to be heated again.

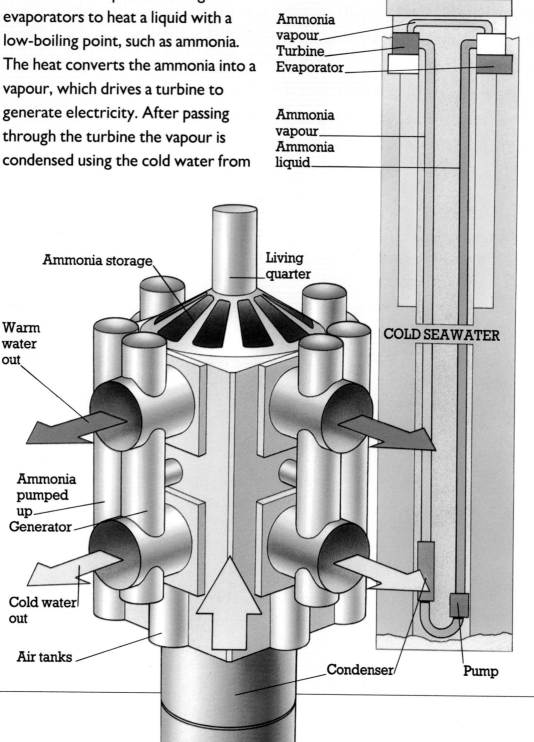

Ammonia vapour
Turbine
Evaporator
Ammonia vapour
Ammonia liquid
Ammonia storage
Living quarter
COLD SEAWATER
Warm water out
Ammonia pumped up
Generator
Cold water out
Air tanks
Condenser
Pump

WAVE POWER

Waves contain a tremendous amount of energy, as we can see from the damage they sometimes do. Much research has been carried out to find ways of harnessing this energy and putting it to good use. Particular interest is being shown in the use of wave power to provide electricity for isolated islands. Several designs have been successfully tested on a small scale, and some small systems are already in use. Large-scale designs should work just as well. But a system producing the same sort of energy as a large power station would have to be 20 or 30 kilometres long and it would also need to be strong enough to withstand the battering effects of storms. People might not like having such a large and unsightly structure spoiling the beauty of the coastline.

AIR BAGS

Many different systems have been developed to make use of wave power. One design uses air-filled bags connected to an air turbine by a series of ducts. When a wave passes over a bag, the water pressure compresses the bag, and forces the air out. The air is directed through the ducts to drive the turbine. When the wave has passed, the bag fills with air again and returns to its original shape, ready for the next wave.

▽ **Design for wave power station**

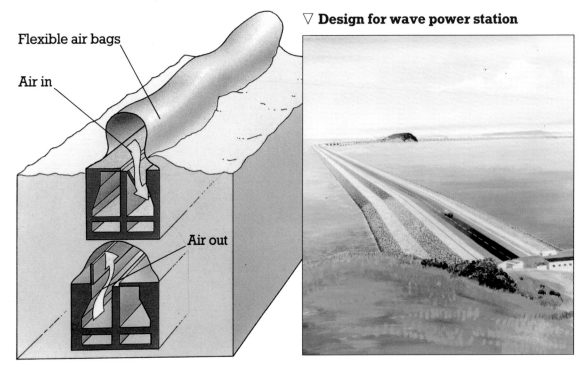

Flexible air bags

Air in

Air out

THE NODDING DUCK

Wave power can also be harnessed by a series of floats shaped like rounded wedges. The floats are carried on a fixed central section so they rock up and down with the waves (like ducks bobbing on water). The rocking motion is used to drive pumps, which push water along the central section to a turbine. The turbine could turn gyroscopes (spinning wheels) that would store the energy and give an even power output, despite variations in the waves.

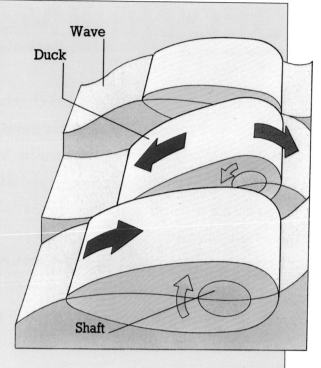

CONTOURING RAFT

This design uses floating rafts, which are joined together so that the parts can move like doors on a hinge as waves pass beneath them. Special pumps are fitted between the rafts. The movement of the rafts expands and compresses the pumps, drawing fluid in or forcing it out. The moving fluid is then used to drive a turbine to generate electricity.

GEOTHERMAL

As you go deeper into the Earth, the temperature of the rocks gets hotter and hotter. The heat is partly left over from the time when the Earth was formed, and partly from the decay of radioactive materials in the rocks. Geothermal energy can be obtained from this natural supply of heat. In some areas, the heat comes to the surface in the form of hot springs. Sources of this type have been exploited for many years. At first they just provided heating, but eventually the energy was controlled in order to generate electricity. The first geothermal power station was built in Italy over 80 years ago. Methods have also been developed to use the heat from dry rocks. The Wairakei plant in New Zealand produces a tenth of the countries electricity.

GEOTHERMAL SPRINGS

In certain areas the rock near the surface of the Earth is particularly hot. Any water passing through the rock heats up, and may emerge as a hot spring. Where the temperature is particularly high, some of the water may turn to steam, and the water is forced out as a geyser.

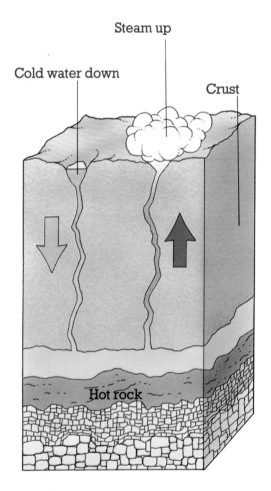

Steam up

Cold water down

Crust

Hot rock

◁ Lady Knox geyser, New Zealand

GEOTHERMAL POWER STATION

Hot dry rocks can also be used as a source of energy. Holes are drilled into the ground and explosives used to crack the rock. Water is pumped down one of the holes, is heated as it travels through the cracked rock, and comes out of the other hole as steam.

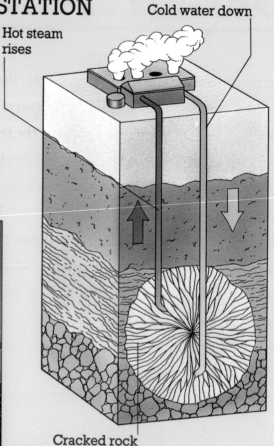

Cold water down

Hot steam rises

Cracked rock

◁ Thermal power station
(See also below)

ICELAND

In Iceland, hot spring water and heat extracted from solidified lava flows are a major source of energy. About 70 per cent of homes are heated this way, and it is even possible to heat greenhouses to grow tropical vegetables and fruit. Geothermal energy in Iceland is also used in industry and for generating electricity.

GREEN ENERGY

Until coal came into general use, wood had been the main source of fuel for thousands of years. In some countries it still supplies up to 90 per cent of the energy used. Biofuels – the term used for wood and other organic materials – provide around 15 per cent of the world's energy needs. Plants are particularly efficient because they trap the Sun's energy directly and, if they are managed properly, are a true renewable energy source. In some areas, however, plant resources are being used up rapidly and are not being replaced. Most biofuels provide energy by being burnt, but this way of using them is not always convenient. So methods are now being found to process biofuels into forms such as gas and oil, which can be used for more varied purposes.

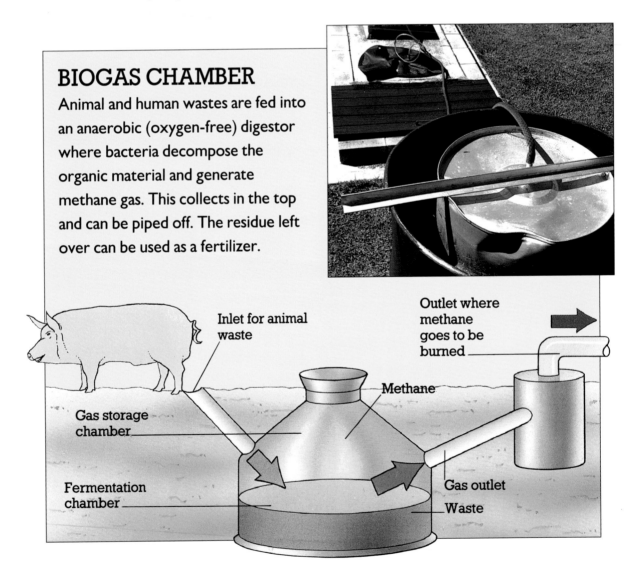

BIOGAS CHAMBER

Animal and human wastes are fed into an anaerobic (oxygen-free) digestor where bacteria decompose the organic material and generate methane gas. This collects in the top and can be piped off. The residue left over can be used as a fertilizer.

Inlet for animal waste

Outlet where methane goes to be burned

Methane

Gas storage chamber

Fermentation chamber

Gas outlet

Waste

ORGANIC FUEL

Plants such as maize, cassava and sugar cane can be fermented to produce alcohol, which can be used as a fuel. Biofuels, such as peat (semi-decayed plant material) and wood, give off energy through burning, but collecting them is very time-consuming.

△ Cutting peat in Ireland
▽ Collecting firewood in India

BIOREACTORS

Refuse may be used in bioreactors. These systems grow algae and bacteria on organic materials, and produce gases and other energy-rich materials. Industry may use methane piped directly from refuse dumps.

Maize

Cassava

Sugar cane

18 ENERGY FROM SPACE

Nearly half of the energy from the Sun is absorbed by the atmosphere before it reaches the Earth. One way of avoiding this loss is to collect the power in space. A satellite power station could be put in orbit above the Earth, and kept permanently in place over a ground station. Because of its size the satellite would have to be built in space, and would require huge launchers to transport the parts. Large numbers of solar panels would trap the Sun's light and convert its energy into electricity. The electricity would be sent to the ground stations as microwave radiation. This can travel through the atmosphere much more easily than heat radiation. At the ground station, the microwaves would be collected by aerials and converted back into electricity.

GIANT SATELLITES

Satellite power stations would have to be built on an enormous scale, with up to 100 square kilometres of solar cells. One of the disadvantages of this system is that getting such a satellite into space might take half as much energy as it would ever produce! On the ground, the receiving station would cover a large area, and would need a big safety zone around it.

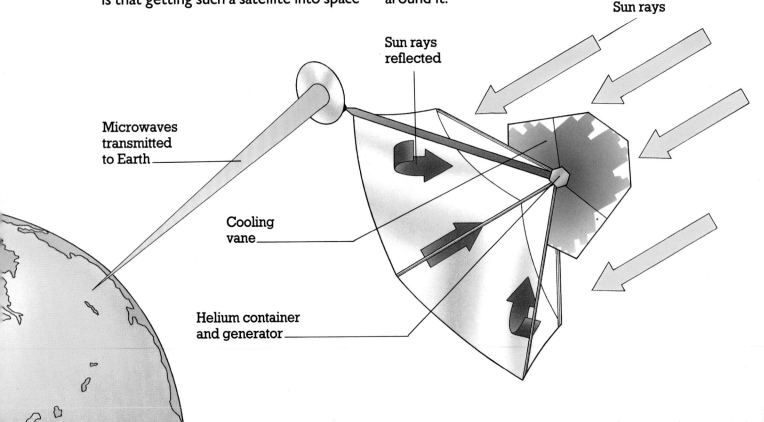

Sun rays

Sun rays reflected

Microwaves transmitted to Earth

Cooling vane

Helium container and generator

FUEL FOR TRANSPORT

Transport accounts for around a fifth of the energy we use. Finding alternative fuels is urgent because oil supplies are starting to run out. At the moment, oil provides over 90 per cent of transport fuel. Oil fuels are so popular because they are a very concentrated form of energy and are particularly easy to handle and store; replacement fuels would ideally have the same properties. Possible options include synthetic oils made from fossil fuels such as coal or biomass fuels – fuels from plant material that was recently living, such as wood or sugar cane. Increasing use may also be made of electricity to power the transport of the future. Some of these options have the additional advantage of causing less pollution than present types of fuel and engine.

ELECTRIC POWERED CARS

The weight and limited storage capacity of present-day batteries restrict the performance of electric cars. Improved batteries should be able to overcome these problems, especially for use in towns. Some recent designs that use battery power also have a small petrol engine to give a greater range of speeds.

General Motors Impact
electric car

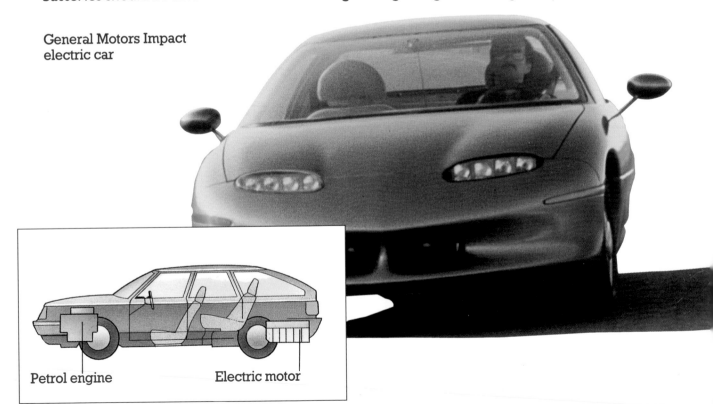

Petrol engine   Electric motor

△ Prototype car running on mixture of methanol and hydrogen

OTHER FUEL ALTERNATIVES

Hydrogen is a convenient fuel to use, but it takes a great deal of energy to produce it. For use in cars, hydrogen gas would be liquefied by cooling it to a very low temperature, and then stored in heavily insulated tanks. Alcohol produced by fermenting crops such as sugar cane and maize is already being used to fuel motor vehicles. It can be used on its own in special engines or, if it is mixed with petrol to make "gasahol", it can power normal petrol engines.

▽ Filling station with alcohol and petrol

STORING ENERGY

One of the problems with many alternative types of energy is that the power can only be produced under the right conditions, and they do not always arise when the energy is needed. To make the best use of these energy sources we need to be able to store the power and release it as required. Storage systems can also be used to help meet sudden peaks in demand, and thus run generating plants at the highest possible efficiency. Most systems work by converting electricity into another form of energy, which is converted back when the power is needed. Batteries provide suitable storage for small amounts of power, such as the excess output from a single wind generator, but other systems will be needed for large-scale use.

FUEL CELL

Fuel cells produce electricity by combining a fuel, hydrogen, with an oxidizer, oxygen. In a simple design, the oxygen and hydrogen are fed into porous electrodes separated by an electrolyte solution. Reactions at the electrodes generate electricity. For energy storage, electricity is used to electrolyse water and the hydrogen and oxygen generated are collected and stored for later use in a fuel cell.

▽ Fuel cell in Manhattan, U.S.A.

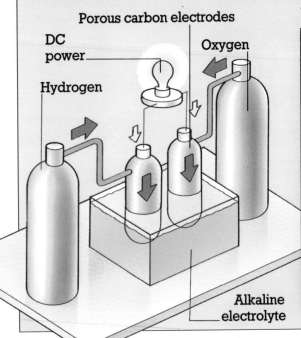

Porous carbon electrodes

DC power

Oxygen

Hydrogen

Alkaline electrolyte

FLYWHEEL

High-speed flywheels can store a lot of power as kinetic energy – energy in the form of motion. They are driven up to speed by electric motors and kept spinning on low-friction bearings until the power is needed. The motors are then driven by the flywheels and act as generators. For safety, flywheels are installed in pits.

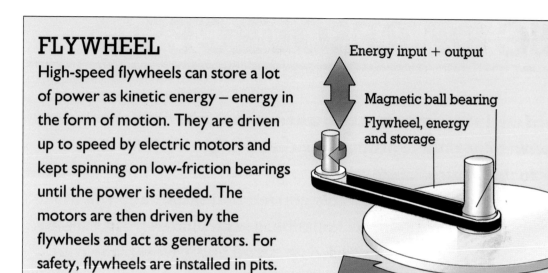

Energy input + output

Magnetic ball bearing

Flywheel, energy and storage

PUMPED STORAGE

Pumped storage schemes are used to balance the supply of electricity. When surplus power is available, it is used to pump water from a low level to a high level reservoir. The water is then released through turbines, giving a rapid output to meet peak demands.

▽ Pumped storage lake, U.K.

Upper reservoir

Surge tunnel

Power house

Lower reservoir

Water flows down at peak demand

Water pumped up when demand is low

USE OF RESOURCES

Established sources such as coal and nuclear power will continue to make an important contribution to our energy needs for the foreseeable future. Large resources for both are known to exist, but these supplies are not renewable and increasing demand will make it important to make the best possible use of whatever is available. As the richer coal seams are used up, small and lower-grade coal deposits would have to be brought into use by improved extraction methods. Increasing use will also have to be made of processes that convert coal into gas and oil in order to meet the specific requirements of industry and transport. At the same time, the introduction of new and improved ways of using fuels will increase efficiency and help to reduce pollution.

FAST BREEDER

Although uranium is widely distributed, less than one per cent of it is the U-235 isotope that can be used in nuclear fission reactors. Fast breeder reactors can convert the far more common U-238 into plutonium, which can also be used as a reactor fuel. The U-238 is placed in the reactor core, and is converted when it absorbs radiation produced by the fission process.

▽ Loading fuel into a reactor

COAL TO GAS

Coal reserves that are difficult to reach may be exploited by converting the coal to gas while still underground. Shafts are dug down to the coal seam and the coal set alight. Carefully controlled amounts of oxygen or air are pumped in so the coal only partly burns. The gas can then be piped to the surface.

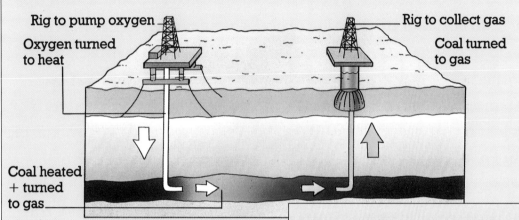

Rig to pump oxygen
Oxygen turned to heat
Coal heated + turned to gas

Rig to collect gas
Coal turned to gas

PETROL FROM COAL

There are a number of established processes for producing petrol and other oil fuels from coal. Most of the petrol used in South Africa is produced in chemical plants as the country has no oil of its own, but plenty of coal. The plants can produce more than three million tonnes of oil every year.

▽ Petrol from coal, S. Africa

FLUIDIZED BED

A fluidized bed furnace gives efficient coal burning for heating water. Air is blown through a bed of material that does not burn. This makes it float. Powdered coal is blown into the bed, where burning takes place.

Fluidized bed furnace
Hot gases
Cold water
Steam
Burning coal
Air
Ash

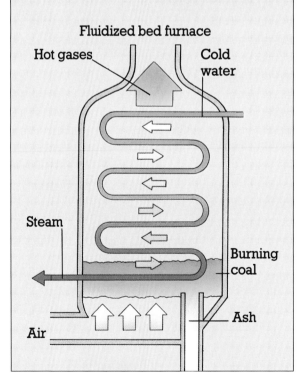

ENERGY FROM WASTE

About 60 per cent of household waste (including paper) is organic material with a substantial energy content. At the moment, very little use is made of this. When rubbish is disposed of in landfill tips it starts to rot, and this rotting process generates methane. A build-up of this gas could cause a large explosion so it must be safely controlled. The gas from large tips is collected and piped off to supply industry or used for local heating. On small tips, the gas is often just burnt off. Another way of recovering energy from waste is to burn it and use the heat produced to heat houses, etc, to generate electricity, or in industry. Alternatively, the rubbish can be pulverised, the materials that will not burn taken out, and the remaining matter processed into fuel pellets.

RECYCLING

Efficient recycling removes useful materials before waste is disposed of. Recoverable materials include metals, glass and, in some cases, plastic.

Recycling not only helps conserve resources; the process also saves energy since less power is needed to reprocess the materials than to extract and refine fresh supplies.

▽ Landfill dump

WASTE TO ELECTRICITY

The main reason for burning rubbish is to dispose of it more efficiently, the remaining ash takes up less than a third of the original volume. The heat produced in some incinerators, however, is also used to produce steam to generate electricity.

△ Burning waste to generate electricity
▽ Methane gas plant beside tip

HOME HEATING

Integrated waste disposal and heating systems may be possible in densely-populated areas. Waste is transported by pipe to the processing plant, where it is sorted and burnt. Heat from the furnace provides central heating.

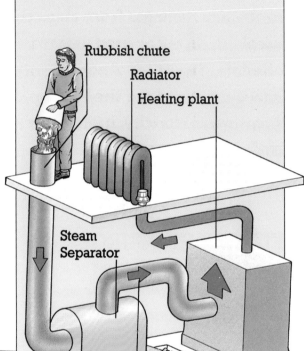

Rubbish chute
Radiator
Heating plant
Steam Separator
Paper and burnable rubbish
Glass + metal

USING ENERGY WISELY

Finding and developing new energy sources is only part of the solution to our long-term energy needs. Making proper use of the energy we have is just as important. Effective energy conservation could considerably extend the life of existing fuel resources, and make the introduction of new sources much less urgent. The necessary techniques for conserving energy are now well established, the next step is to ensure that they are used as much as possible. There are a number of ways to persuade people to save energy. In the USA, energy suppliers have started to pay consumers to improve their insulation and therefore reduce their energy consumption. This costs the suppliers less than installing new generators to increase production.

FUTURE RESOURCES

Our future energy needs will be supplied by a combination of many different sources, ranging from nuclear reactors to small wind and water wheels that provide power for a single house. Computer control systems will integrate the performance of all these systems to make sure as much power as possible comes from low-cost and renewable sources. As alternative sources become more widely available, small-scale systems meeting local needs may start to replace current large-scale central power stations. These stations are often the most efficient way of producing electricity, but do not always make the best overall use of energy. For example using waste heat from a power station for local heating can raise the overall efficiency to more than 70 per cent.

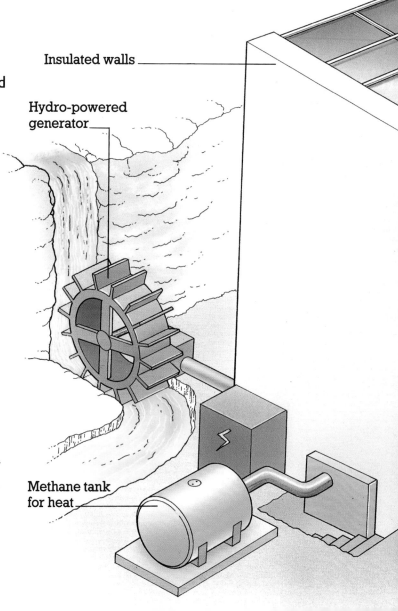

Insulated walls

Hydro-powered generator

Methane tank for heat

FUTURE HOUSES

Houses designed to make the best possible use of energy can minimize heat loss through high levels of insulation and good draught-proofing. Recovery systems use heat from stale air to heat fresh air before it gets into the house, and they also save the heat from waste water. The south-facing windows trap solar energy.

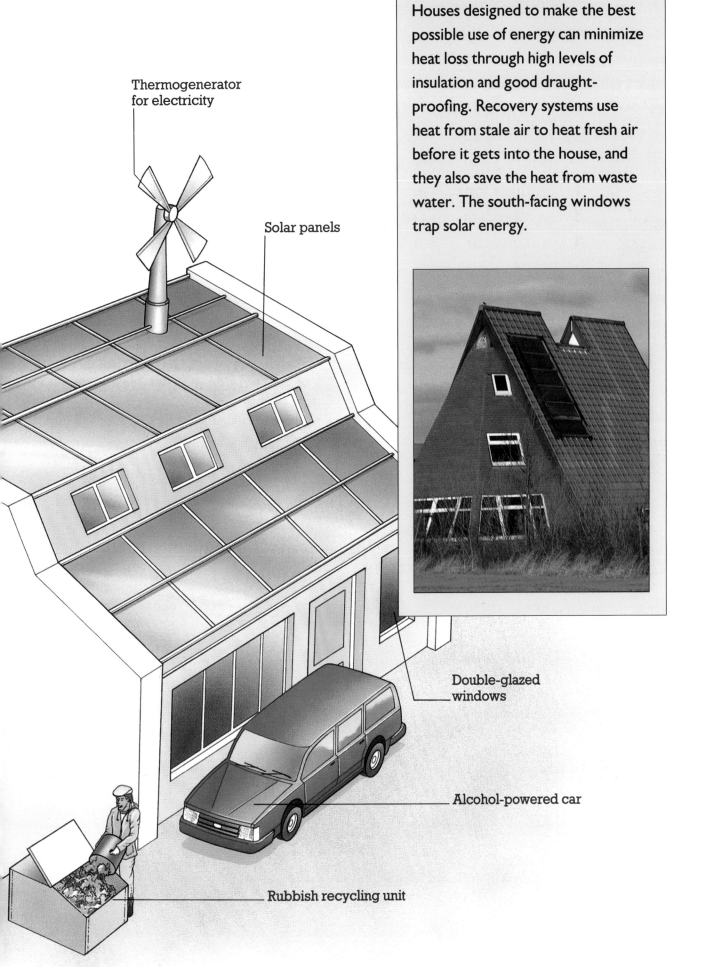

Thermogenerator for electricity

Solar panels

Double-glazed windows

Alcohol-powered car

Rubbish recycling unit

WORLD ENERGY USE

In the mid 1980s, world energy consumption was approximately equivalent to the energy in 7.5 thousand million tonnes of oil. Oil itself accounted for 35 per cent of this; coal 30 per cent; natural gas 20 per cent; and the remaining 15 per cent came from a variety of sources, including hydroelectricity, nuclear power and biofuels.

The average world energy consumption is about 2 kilowatts per person each day. North Americans use about five times this average, Europeans twice the average, and some African and Asian countries less than a tenth of the average. Although some developed countries are much more efficient than others in their use of energy, in general, the amount of energy used by a country rises with its standard of living. Demand increases as more people drive their own cars and as their homes become more comfortable, with central heating, labour-saving devices, etc.

The chart shows how much energy different areas of the world use. But different areas have different populations. For example, the population of China is four times greater than that of North America, but China uses only a quarter as much energy. If each person in China used as much energy as the average North American, China would use as much as the rest of the world put together.

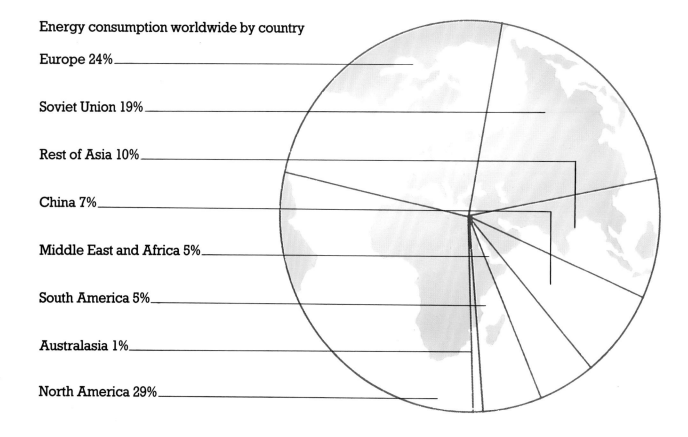

Energy consumption worldwide by country

Europe 24%

Soviet Union 19%

Rest of Asia 10%

China 7%

Middle East and Africa 5%

South America 5%

Australasia 1%

North America 29%

GLOSSARY

anaerobic digester apparatus for producing methane through bacterial decay with no oxygen present.

electrolysis process of splitting water into hydrogen and oxygen by passing an electric current through it.

fossil fuels oil, coal and natural gas, formed by the decay of vegetation.

gasahol motor fuel consisting of a mixture of petrol with about 20 per cent ethyl alcohol.

generator machine for converting mechanical energy into electricity.

geyser spring that blows hot water and steam up into the air.

global warming increase of the average temperature of the Earth due to the production of "greenhouse" gases such as carbon dioxide. These gases hold heat in instead of letting it radiate out of the atmosphere.

megawatt (MW) one million watts.

microwave electromagnetic radiation with a wavelength from 0.5 to 30 centimetres.

plasma gas completely ionized so that it consists of free electrons and positive ions.

renewable energy energy from sources that are not used up, such as the Sun, or from sources that are renewed, such as plant material.

watt unit of power. A one-bar electric fire uses 1000 watts. Energy is measured in watt-hours.

Useful addresses

National Power
Sudbury House
15 Newgate Street
London EC1A 7AU
Tel: 071 634 5111

Energy Efficiency Office
Department of Energy
Thames House South
Millbank
London SW1P 4QJ
Tel: 071 238 3000

Friends of the Earth
26-28 Underwood Street
London N1 7JQ
Tel: 071 490 1555

National Centre for Alternative Technology
Llwyngwern Quarry
Machynlleth
Powys

Urban Centre for Appropriate Technology
82 Colston Street
Bristol BS1 5BB

INDEX